Original title:
One Step at a Time

Copyright © 2024 Swan Charm
All rights reserved.

Author: Paula Raudsepp
ISBN HARDBACK: 978-9916-89-748-5
ISBN PAPERBACK: 978-9916-89-749-2
ISBN EBOOK: 978-9916-89-750-8

## Grace in Each Measured Breath

In silence, blessings softly flow,
Breath by breath, our spirits grow.
With every exhale, peace we find,
A sacred rhythm, heart and mind.

Whispers of love in morning light,
Each dawn renews our inner sight.
With gratitude, we rise and share,
A dance of grace, a humble prayer.

Embrace the stillness, seek the gold,
In every moment, stories told.
A tapestry of hope and faith,
In every breath, divine embrace.

## The Mosaic of Continuous Belief

Fragments of faith in colors bright,
Each piece a star in the darkest night.
Bound together through trials faced,
In every heart, the love is traced.

From ancient texts to whispered dreams,
A journey woven in sacred streams.
Each thought a thread, a binding tie,
In every challenge, we learn to fly.

A harmony of voices blend,
Unity found in hands we lend.
In this mosaic, we find our place,
The beauty of life, a gift of grace.

## Each Step a Testimony

With every footfall on this path,
We carry stories that heal and last.
In trials faced, our spirits soar,
Each step a testament, forevermore.

The journey unfolds with purpose clear,
In shadows cast, we conquer fear.
With hearts awake, we tread with care,
In faith, we find the strength to bear.

Every moment, a lesson learned,
In love's embrace, our souls are turned.
Through valleys deep and mountains high,
Each step a song, our spirits fly.

## The Unseen Guide of Compassion

In quiet moments, we feel the call,
An unseen guide that nurtures all.
Through acts of kindness, love flows free,
Compassion blooms, a sacred tree.

With gentle hands, we touch the heart,
Embracing souls, never apart.
Each gesture we make, a bridge we build,
In unity, our spirits are filled.

The warmth of presence, a light to share,
In every struggle, we show we care.
With open arms, we welcome grace,
The unseen guide in every place.

## Clarity in the Wilderness Walk

In shadows deep, His light does shine,
Guiding the lost with love divine.
Through paths unknown, His hand I trace,
In every step, I find His grace.

Each whisper soft, a truth to hold,
In barren lands, His warmth is gold.
The tangled thoughts begin to clear,
As faith unfolds, I draw Him near.

The silence speaks in holy rhyme,
In solitude, we dance with time.
Each moment spent, a sacred gift,
In wilderness, my soul does lift.

With every trial, I stand renewed,
In doubt's embrace, His peace imbued.
A steadfast heart, my humble plea,
In wilderness, I walk with Thee.

## The Harmony of His Calling

In gentle tones, He calls my name,
A melody that breaks the shame.
With every note, my spirit soars,
In harmony, my heart restores.

Through trials loud, His song prevails,
A symphony that never fails.
In each refrain, I find my place,
Embraced by love, a warm embrace.

The rhythms weave like threads of gold,
In every beat, His truth unfolds.
With open ears, I hear His will,
In harmony, my heart is still.

From valleys low to mountains high,
His cadence flows, I cannot lie.
In every step, I feel His grace,
In harmony, I find my space.

## The Stepping Stones of Grace

Each stone I tread, a path defined,
In every step, His love aligned.
Across the brook, through fields of light,
The stones of faith guide me in flight.

With every leap, I find the way,
A bridge of hope in break of day.
Firm ground beneath, His promise stands,
The stones of grace in sacred hands.

Through storms that rage and winds that blow,
My feet are planted, peace does flow.
In trials faced, my heart does brace,
Each stone a word of His embrace.

On this journey, I stand secure,
The path ahead is bright and pure.
With eyes on Him, I claim my place,
Each step I take, a gift of grace.

## Baby Steps to Eternity

With tiny feet, I learn to walk,
In faith so small, yet strong as rock.
Each step I take, a trust renewed,
In every breath, my spirit's view.

The world ahead seems vast and wide,
Yet in His arms, I safely bide.
With every fall, He lifts my head,
In every tear, His love is spread.

In moments small, the light expands,
As I embark on foreign lands.
The journey long, yet closer still,
In baby steps, I seek His will.

With every heartbeat, time unfolds,
The tale of grace that He has told.
In fluttering beats, I find my way,
In baby steps, I choose to sway.

## The Tranquility of Trusting Steps

In the silence of the dawn, we tread,
With faith as our guide, no fear to spread.
Each step a whisper, each breath a prayer,
In the heart of trust, we find Him there.

Paths unseen, yet brightly lit,
With every move, our worries sit.
The ground we walk, a sacred place,
In His embrace, we find our grace.

Through valleys deep, and mountains high,
We lift our hands, we learn to fly.
In tranquility, we find our peace,
As trusting steps grant our fears release.

Together we journey, hand in hand,
With love as the light, we make our stand.
In unity strong, our voices rise,
An anthem of hope that fills the skies.

For in this path of faith we tread,
With open hearts, where angels led.
We walk in trust, our burdens light,
In the tranquility of His guiding light.

## The Footpath of Forgiveness

Along the path where shadows fade,
Forgiveness blossoms, love displayed.
We lift the weight of bitter chains,
To walk in peace where love remains.

With gentle hearts, we make amends,
In sacred bonds, where healing bends.
Each step anew, a chance to mend,
In the light of grace, our spirits blend.

Through trials faced and hearts once torn,
We find the strength, reborn, reborn.
In every word that we release,
We pave the way for lasting peace.

So let us tread this hallowed ground,
Where mercy flows, and hope is found.
The footpath calls with gentle grace,
Each step a brush with Heaven's face.

In forgiveness deep, our souls unite,
Together we shine, a radiant light.
May our hearts echo the love we seek,
On the footpath pure, where spirits speak.

## Illuminated by His Promises

In the quiet of the night, we dream,
Illuminated by His gentle beam.
Promises whispered, softly heard,
In faith's embrace, we find His word.

The stars above, a guiding light,
Reminding us of grace each night.
Through storms and trials, He leads us home,
In every step, we need not roam.

Through valleys dark, His light will shine,
In every heartbeat, His love divine.
Each promise made a thread of gold,
A tapestry of truth to behold.

With every dawn, new hope will rise,
In the beauty of His boundless skies.
Illuminated paths before our eyes,
A journey rich with endless ties.

In thankfulness, we lift our praise,
For His promises that guide our ways.
With open hearts, we walk as one,
In His brilliance, life has just begun.

## As the Spirit Moves

As the spirit moves, we hear the call,
In silent moments, we surrender all.
With open hearts and willing hands,
We journey forth, where love expands.

In unity, we find our strength,
Embracing all at every length.
The spirit dances within our soul,
In harmony, we find our goal.

Through trials faced, His grace will flow,
In every heartbreak, love will grow.
We trust the path His spirit shows,
Through every bend, our faith bestows.

In whispered prayers, we find our way,
As light reveals the dawn of day.
Together, we will rise anew,
Creating joy in all we do.

With every breath, we sing His song,
As the spirit moves, we all belong.
In this journey, united we find,
The beauty of love, a gift so kind.

## The Incremental Dance of Hope

In shadows deep, a whisper stirs,
The heart awakens, lost dreams confer.
With every step, the light grows strong,
A melody woven, a timeless song.

In moments small, faith gently sways,
Embracing the dawn of brighter days.
When tears like rivers start to flow,
Hope's soft rhythm begins to grow.

The dance of grace in silent nights,
Guides weary souls toward heavenly sights.
Each breath a promise, each sigh a prayer,
In the incremental quest, we find what's rare.

As stars align in the cosmic sea,
Our hearts unite, we dance with glee.
Each spark ignites the path we tread,
In hope's embrace, the spirit is fed.

Through trials faced and burdens shared,
The dance of hope shows we are cared.
Together we rise, we strive, we stand,
In unity's grace, we join His hand.

## **Beyond the Horizon's Embrace**

Across the fields where shadows play,
The sun awakens, heralds the day.
With every breath, a promise assured,
Beyond the horizon, love is secured.

In quiet whispers, nature sings,
Of distant hopes and angelic wings.
With steadfast hearts, we seek the light,
Guided by faith through the longest night.

Where dreams are stitched with threads of gold,
A prayer emerges, both brave and bold.
In stillness found, our spirits soar,
Beyond the horizon, we yearn for more.

Through valleys deep and mountains high,
We chase the truth, both low and nigh.
In unity, we rise above,
To find our place in endless love.

Beyond the horizon, where mercy flows,
In every heart, the light still glows.
With open arms, the world we face,
Together forever, in His grace.

## Prayers in the Pace of Life

In the bustle of dawn's awakening,
We find His presence, gently shaking.
Each moment cherished, a sacred gift,
In the prayers we speak, our spirits lift.

With every heartbeat, our souls align,
In the pace of life, His love we find.
Among the chaos, peace unfolds,
In whispered vows, our faith upholds.

Through trials faced, on paths unknown,
We seek the light that can be shown.
In quiet moments, our hearts entwine,
In prayerful whispers, His love divine.

As seasons change and time flows on,
Our prayers endure, a steadfast song.
In every sorrow, in all delight,
We journey forth, guided by light.

Life's tender dance, a rhythm pure,
In prayers we find, our spirits mature.
With hands uplifted, we walk in grace,
In the pace of life, we find our place.

## The Subtle Call of Sacred Steps

In quiet corners where echoes dwell,
The subtle call begins to swell.
With each soft step, a journey starts,
Where sacred whispers speak to hearts.

Through wooded paths and rivers wide,
The sacred call, our faithful guide.
Each footfall gentle, each breath a prayer,
In the stillness found, we kneel in care.

Across the meadows, where spirits tread,
With every heartbeat, we forge ahead.
In unity's song, together we climb,
The sacred steps, transcendental and sublime.

In every moment, His grace we trace,
Beyond the veil of time and space.
In sacred rhythms, our souls rejoice,
With every whisper, we hear His voice.

As dawn breaks forth and shadows flee,
We walk the path He's set for thee.
In the subtle call, we heed His way,
In sacred steps, forever we'll stay.

## Embracing the Divine Rhythm

In silence we hear the whispers,
Of grace that flows through time.
Hearts lifted in sweet surrender,
Awake to the rhythm sublime.

In the dance of light and shadow,
We find our steps aligned.
Each heartbeat a sacred echo,
In stillness, our souls entwined.

With every breath, we proclaim,
The love that knows no bounds.
In the joy and the pain,
The divine presence surrounds.

As stars grace the evening sky,
So too does His mercy shine.
In every tear we cry,
A sign of love divine.

Together, we journey as one,
In the heartbeat of the night.
With hope and faith, we run,
Toward the eternal light.

## A Heartbeat Away from Purpose

In the stillness, we listen close,
To the calling deep inside.
A heartbeat away, we approach,
The purpose where dreams abide.

Each step guided by the vision,
A path laid out in grace.
With faith as our strong decision,
We courageously embrace.

In moments of doubt and fear,
He walks beside us still.
A heartbeat away, He is near,
With love that will fulfill.

Through trials that life may send,
Our spirits rise above.
In Him, we find our friend,
In each act of love.

Together we seek the light,
In the dance of day and night.
With hearts beating in unity,
We find our sacred right.

## The Tapestry of Daily Devotion

Thread by thread, we weave our prayer,
In moments both small and grand.
A tapestry of devotion rare,
In the Master's loving hand.

With gratitude, we tell our tale,
In each act, both great and meek.
Through joy and sorrow, we shall prevail,
His wisdom is what we seek.

The colors blend in harmony,
Each life a unique design.
In His light, we find unity,
Our spirits forever align.

From sunrise to twilight's glow,
We offer our hearts anew.
In every moment, we sow,
The seeds of faith that grew.

As we gather, our voices raise,
In a chorus of love's embrace.
The tapestry of our days,
Reflects His eternal grace.

## **Steadfast Through the Storm**

In tempest's roar, we find our peace,
Anchored by faith's embrace.
Through trials, our spirits increase,
In His unchanging grace.

With every wave that crashes near,
Our hearts hold firm in trust.
For in the storm, He draws us near,
Our refuge, strong and just.

Though darkness tries to steal our light,
In Him, our hope remains.
Through sleepless nights and lonely fights,
We rise above the chains.

With every breath, we claim His name,
A shield against the night.
Through fire and flood, we'll never wane,
In love, we find our might.

Together we stand, hands held high,
In unity, we'll prevail.
Steadfast through storms that test the sky,
We shine, we never fail.

## The Journey of a Thousand Hearts

In a land where shadows fade,
A thousand hearts begin to tread.
With each step, a prayer is made,
Finding light where hope is fed.

Through valleys deep and mountains high,
Their voices rise like morning's song.
With faith as wings, they touch the sky,
United, where they all belong.

On paths of love, they walk as one,
Dancing in the grace of light.
Their journey shines like the sun,
Illuminating darkest night.

With every trial, strength they find,
In every tear, a lesson learned.
Compassion, in their hearts entwined,
A flame of hope forever burned.

As the stars begin to gleam,
Their spirits rise, no longer bound.
Together in a common dream,
A harmony, profound and sound.

## Gracefully Wading Through Life's Stream

In the gentle flow of time,
We wade through waters deep and wide.
Trusting Love, our guiding rhyme,
Where faith and grace do gently guide.

With each ripple, lessons flow,
Stories told in every wave.
In turbulent tides, we learn to grow,
By sacred hands, we are so brave.

Through stormy skies or sunny days,
We find our way with hearts aglow.
In quiet moments, we give praise,
For every step, His love we know.

Stepping lightly, hearts in sync,
Together in this sacred stream.
With faith as anchor, never sink,
Embracing life, a holy dream.

As echoes fade and waters clear,
We find tranquility in our song.
In every heart, He draws us near,
In this stream of love, we belong.

## A Pilgrim's Progress in Prayer

On a winding road, a pilgrim treads,
With a heart that seeks the divine.
In each whispered prayer, hope spreads,
A light that leads, forever shines.

Through shadows cast by doubt and fear,
The pilgrim stands with open hands.
In silent moments, He draws near,
In sacred trust, each step withstands.

From valleys low to mountain peaks,
In every breath, a chance to pray.
With humble heart, the pilgrim seeks,
To walk in truth, to find the way.

Amidst the trials, spirits soar,
With every prayer, a path unfolds.
Each tear and smile, a sacred score,
In God's embrace, the heart beholds.

With joy renewed in every turn,
The pilgrim walks with strengthened grace.
In silent prayers, our spirits burn,
Through every mile, we seek His face.

## Ascending the Mount of Belief

With weary feet, we climb the height,
Each step a prayer, each breath a hymn.
The summit calls, a beacon bright,
As hearts uplift, though shadows dim.

Through trials faced and fears confronted,
We rise with faith, a steadfast crew.
In every moment, hope is planted,
A tapestry of love in view.

The mount reveals what lies within,
A sacred truth, a light divine.
With open hearts, we shed our sin,
Bound together, our paths align.

As we ascend, our spirits soar,
In quiet reverence, we believe.
With joyous hearts, we seek for more,
In grace and mercy, we receive.

Atop the mount, we stand as one,
Embracing love that breaks all chains.
In every battle fought and won,
With faith, we weave eternal gains.

## Steps on Holy Ground

Upon this sacred place we tread,
With humble hearts and spirits led.
Each step a prayer, each breath a song,
In reverence deep, where we belong.

Angels whisper, guiding our way,
In golden light, they softly sway.
With every footfall, blessings flow,
The holy path we come to know.

Devotion blooms like flowers in spring,
In silent peace, our souls take wing.
We seek the truth that's ever near,
In faith's embrace, we lose our fear.

The earth beneath our feet is blessed,
In trials faced, our hearts find rest.
A journey shared, no soul alone,
In love divine, we find our home.

With every step, the spirit's tune,
Resounding softly, morning to noon.
Here on this holy ground we stand,
United in love, hand in hand.

## **Guided by Celestial Light**

In twilight veils, the stars do gleam,
A beacon bright, a guiding dream.
We walk in faith, through shadows cast,
With hearts aflame, our fears surpassed.

Celestial light, so pure and bright,
Illuminates our path each night.
Through valleys deep, and mountains high,
We follow where the Spirit's nigh.

Each whispered prayer, a gentle call,
In every stumble, we shall not fall.
For in the depth of darkest days,
Our hearts ignite with sacred rays.

In trust we find the strength to soar,
With every step, we yearn for more.
For every journey leads us hence,
To realms of peace, and recompense.

A purpose grand, we seek to share,
In acts of love, a holy care.
With faith as guide, our souls take flight,
Forever blessed by Celestial light.

## Faithful Footprints on Earth

With every footprint in the clay,
We leave our mark along the way.
In kindness shared and love bestowed,
Our faithful hearts, they've surely glowed.

The earth a canvas, our lives a sign,
In every act of grace divine.
Where tears have fallen, and joy has spread,
In faith we rise, while others tread.

From trials faced, new strength is drawn,
In breaking dawn, we greet the morn.
These footprints tell of battles won,
In unity, we've always run.

Each step we take a testament,
Of love unbound, of time well spent.
In thoughtful grace, our souls awake,
To weave a path for others' sake.

Together in this earthly dance,
Our faithful journeys lead a chance.
In every heart, a light will shine,
As faithful footprints intertwine.

## The Journey of the Pilgrim Soul

Across the lands, we roam and seek,
The whispers of the spirit speak.
In every heart, a pilgrim's plea,
To find the truth, to set it free.

With burdens lifted, we take our stride,
In faith's embrace, we walk with pride.
The journey long, yet sweet and bold,
In stories shared, our hearts behold.

From dawn's first light to starry night,
We treasure each moment, pure and bright.
For every lesson learned along,
Is woven deep in nature's song.

We wander forth, through joy and pain,
In every drop of falling rain.
With every step, love's echo calls,
The pilgrim's heart, forever enthralls.

Together bound, our spirits soar,
In search of grace forevermore.
The journey calls, with hope anew,
For pilgrim souls, the sky so blue.

## Landscapes of the Spirit

In valleys deep, the soul does dwell,
Where whispers of the sacred swell.
Mountains rise, a faith-filled flight,
Guiding hearts through day and night.

Rivers flow with grace bestowed,
Each drop a tale of love bestowed.
The sun ignites the morning's hue,
Awakening hope, ever true.

Fields of flowers bow and bend,
In every petal, a divine blend.
Nature sings in harmony,
A testament to unity.

In shadows cast, there lies a spark,
Illuminating even the dark.
With every breath, we seek, we rise,
Revealing realms beyond the skies.

Through landscapes vast, our spirits soar,
To seek the light forevermore.
Each step a prayer, each glance a sign,
In faith and love, our souls entwine.

## The Unseen Roads of Grace

Along the paths where few have walked,
In silence, faith and hope have talked.
The unseen roads of grace unfold,
With stories rich, and truths retold.

In gentle winds, the spirits guide,
As we venture, hand in hand, side by side.
Each twist and turn, a chance to learn,
In faith we trust, and hearts we yearn.

The light that glimmers from afar,
Is but a glimpse of who we are.
On every road, His love awaits,
With open arms, embracing fates.

Through trials faced and joys embraced,
We've forged a bond that won't be erased.
In every step, His mercy flows,
Transforming hearts from inside, it shows.

So take a breath, and walk with grace,
The unseen roads, a holy space.
In every moment, let us be,
United in His love, eternally.

## Witnessing the Wonders in Passage

In fleeting time, we find the signs,
Wonders bloom where love aligns.
Each moment captures, a treasure holds,
Stories of grace, more precious than gold.

The stars above, like prayers ascend,
Whispering dreams, in night they blend.
Mornings break with colors bright,
A canvas painted by heaven's light.

From each encounter, wisdom flows,
In strangers met, divinity shows.
Witnessing wonders, hearts embrace,
In every smile, we meet His grace.

Nature speaks in sacred tones,
In rustling leaves and distant moans.
With open eyes, we can perceive,
The beauty in what we believe.

Through passages where spirits roam,
In every journey, we find our home.
Life's wonders call, let us be still,
For in our hearts, His love we fill.

## Quietude in Each Advance

In quietude, the spirit knows,
The path unfolds as stillness grows.
Each step taken, reverent and slow,
Where faith becomes the gentle flow.

In every breath, a chance to hear,
The whispers soft, the heart draws near.
Guided by peace, we find our way,
Through trials faced, in light of day.

With every pause, the world dissolves,
In sacred silence, deep resolve.
Here in the stillness, we come alive,
The sacred dance in which we thrive.

In steps unhurried, we draw in grace,
As wisdom blooms in every space.
Each advanced footfall, firm and true,
In quietude, we find what's due.

So let us walk with heart in hand,
Towards horizons vast and grand.
In every advance, let love reside,
In quietude, our souls abide.

## **An Ode to Resilience**

In the shadows, courage shines,
Strength rises like the sun.
Through storms and trials, faith entwines,
With every breath, hope is spun.

Mountains tall, yet hearts can soar,
With every fall, we gain our ground.
In the silence, we hear the roar,
Of whispers soft, in love, we're bound.

From ashes, beauty takes its flight,
In darkness, light begins to gleam.
The spirit's spark ignites the night,
In every struggle, there's a dream.

Hands raised high, we face the tide,
With grace and purpose in our stride.
Together, we can turn the tide,
With hearts united, we provide.

So let us walk this path of grace,
With every step, we shed our fears.
In resilience, we find our place,
And shed our doubts through gathered years.

## Each Stride, A Surrender

With each step on this sacred ground,
We lay our burdens at His feet.
In faith, our true strength is found,
As love and mercy gently meet.

Through valleys deep and mountains high,
We walk in trust, we rise above.
In every tear, a silent cry,
Transforms to whispers of His love.

Each stride, a prayer upon the earth,
Each heartbeat echoes heaven's grace.
In surrender, we find rebirth,
As light illumines every space.

As shadows fade and dawn draws near,
Our spirit dances, free and bold.
With gratitude, we cast out fear,
In every moment, love untold.

So let us move with hearts ablaze,
In every step, a sweet refrain.
As we embrace His sacred ways,
Each stride, a surrender to the gain.

## The Divine Compass in My Heart

In the stillness, whispers rise,
A guiding light amidst the dark.
With faith as wings, the spirit flies,
To seek the truth, to leave a mark.

The compass points toward the light,
In shadows deep, it finds its way.
With every trial, renewed insight,
Each choice reflects His love's array.

Through raging storms, through calm and clear,
Our hearts align with every turn.
The divine compass keeps us near,
In every lesson, love we learn.

With open hearts, we seek the call,
In unity, we stand as one.
Through valleys deep, we'll never fall,
For in His grace, the race is run.

So let us follow where He leads,
With hope and joy, we chart our course.
His love sustains our every need,
The compass guides us, a true force.

## **Labors of Love Along the Path**

In every deed, a seed is sown,
With humble hands, we toil and strive.
Through acts of love, our hearts have grown,
In every struggle, we will thrive.

The path is long, with twists and turns,
But in each trial, we find our way.
With every candle's light, hope burns,
A beacon bright, come what may.

With weary feet, yet spirits bold,
We labor on, our purpose clear.
In every heart, a story told,
Of kindness sown, of love sincere.

The weight of love, a gentle grace,
Unites our hearts with every breath.
Through laughter shared, through every embrace,
We conquer doubt, we conquer death.

So let us march with joy and pride,
With every step, a love display.
In labors strong, with faith as guide,
Along the path, we find our way.

## The Slow Burn of Sanctity

In the hush of dawn's embrace,
Whispers of grace begin to trace.
Hearts aflame with love divine,
A gentle glow that starts to shine.

Patience blooms in silent prayer,
Threads of hope woven with care.
Each moment cherished, held so tight,
Transforming darkness into light.

Through trials faced, the spirit grows,
Like ancient trees, their strength bestows.
In shadows deep, the truth remains,
The slow burn of sanctity gains.

With open hands, we offer praise,
In every heartbeat, joy conveys.
We walk the path, though so unsure,
The warmth of love, our souls endure.

So let each flicker fan the flame,
In sacred space, we find our name.
Together bound by faith's sweet turn,
We rise anew from every burn.

## The Quiet Clarity of Faithful Walking

In footsteps light upon the ground,
A sacred journey can be found.
With every step, we seek the way,
In silence deep, His voice will stay.

Through shaded paths and open fields,
The truth reveals what grace now yields.
In gentle moments, wisdom speaks,
With every breath, our spirit seeks.

The quietness holds strength within,
The journey starts where we begin.
With humble hearts and open minds,
We find the peace that love unwinds.

As day turns night, stars shimmer bright,
In faith, we chase the guiding light.
With every stride, doubt fades away,
We walk in trust, come what may.

So let us tread this hallowed ground,
In faithful walking, hope is found.
With every dawn, we shall renew,
A quiet clarity shines through.

## **Weaving a Tapestry of Trust**

Threads of faith in colors bright,
Woven hearts in shared delight.
Each story told, a strand so fine,
Together bound, your soul and mine.

In the loom of life, we take our place,
Intertwined in love's embrace.
With trust, we stitch our dreams with grace,
A tapestry that time can't erase.

Through trials faced and joys that bloom,
In every shadow, we find room.
Each knot we tie strengthens our bond,
In unity, our spirits respond.

So let us weave this cloth of heart,
In every moment, play our part.
With threads of kindness, hope, and care,
A fabric rich, so strong, so rare.

As life unfolds, let love be bold,
In every stitch, a tale retold.
Together we craft this vibrant trust,
A sacred art, a gift that must.

## The Celestial Cartographer

Beneath the stars, a map unfolds,
With sacred lines and tales retold.
Each constellation tells a story,
A journey marked in faith's own glory.

With compass set to guide our way,
In prayerful steps, we find our sway.
The heavens sing in patterned dances,
With every move, divinity chances.

In twilight's hush, the paths align,
The heart's desire, a sacred sign.
With open eyes, we trace the skies,
In starry realms, our spirit flies.

As starlight fades and shadows grow,
The map of life, it's ours to know.
With every turn, we trust the way,
In celestial arms, our souls shall stay.

So let us chart the course with grace,
In every breath, we find our place.
With faith as guide, and love our art,
The celestial cartographer's heart.

**The Ladder to Heaven**


With faith we climb, so high we go,
Each step a prayer, each breath a glow.
The rungs are hope, the strings are grace,
In His embrace, we find our place.

In trials faced, we reach for light,
His love our guide, through darkest night.
Upon this ladder, hearts unveil,
Together strong, we shall not fail.

The angels sing as we ascend,
With every hand, another friend.
The journey long, yet joyful too,
Through faith in Him, our dreams renew.

At Heaven's gate, our souls will soar,
In perfect love, forevermore.
The rungs of hope, a sacred thread,
As one in Him, we'll rise instead.

## Small Steps to Great Change

A whisper soft, a gentle start,
Each small step stirs the faithful heart.
With kindness shared, we start to mend,
From humble acts, great journeys lend.

The seeds we sow, in tender soil,
With faith and love, we share the toil.
Each little deed, a mighty force,
In service found, we stay the course.

Through trials faced, we rise anew,
In every heart, His light shines through.
With every smile, a world unfolds,
In unity, His truth upholds.

From small beginnings, hope shall grow,
Together we reap what love will sow.
In every step, His strength we'll gain,
For small steps lead to great change.

In faith we walk, hand in hand strong,
For in His light, we all belong.
A sacred path, where hearts will bloom,
In every soul, dispels the gloom.

**Anointed by the Sunrise**

Each dawn a gift, a chance to rise,
Awakened hearts beneath the skies.
In golden light, His grace we find,
Renewed each day, His love defined.

The morning breaks, a promise made,
In every ray, His truth displayed.
The clouds disperse, His joy abounds,
In silence, love's sweet whisper sounds.

With open arms, we greet the light,
To shine in darkness, day and night.
In colors bright, His glory beams,
Awakening our deepest dreams.

Anointed, blessed, we rise and go,
Sharing warmth as rivers flow.
With every step, we tell the tale,
In His embrace, we shall not fail.

As sunset falls, our hearts still sing,
For in the night, His love will bring.
A guiding star, forever shines,
With every day, His grace aligns.

## **In the Shadow of His Wings**

In quiet moments, peace we find,
Beneath His wings, our hearts entwined.
The safety found in love's embrace,
In every tear, He leaves His trace.

When storms arise, we need not fear,
For in His arms, we feel Him near.
The whispered prayers, a sacred bond,
In shadows deep, our faith responds.

Through trials faced, we stand secure,
His steadfast love will always endure.
With every heartbeat, strength we gain,
In every sorrow, healing rains.

In darkest nights, He shines so bright,
A guiding hope, our true delight.
Together strong, our spirits soar,
In love's embrace, forevermore.

To trust in Him, a path so clear,
In the shadow of His wings, we hear.
The song of grace that leads us home,
With open hearts, we'll never roam.

## **Paths of Grace**

In the light of dawn, we tread,
With open hearts and minds, we spread.
Each step a whisper, each breath a prayer,
Guided by love, we journey where.

Through valleys low and mountains steep,
In trust we wander, His promise to keep.
The path is painted with colors divine,
In every trial, His glory will shine.

Hands uplifted, we seek His face,
In every moment, we find His grace.
Together we walk, in unity we stand,
The beauty of faith, in our hearts, it's planned.

From shadows deep to sunlight's gleam,
We walk in purpose, held by His dream.
The road ahead is lined with hope,
In divine embrace, our spirits elope.

For every stumble, for every rise,
He lifts our souls, opens our eyes.
In paths of grace, we find our way,
Trusting in Him, come what may.

## The Gentle Whisper of Faith

In silence deep, a voice is heard,
A gentle whisper, like a bird.
Guiding us through the darkest night,
In moments of doubt, He brings us light.

Amidst the chaos, peace we find,
In softest tones, love is kind.
Faith like a river, flowing free,
Enrolls our hearts in harmony.

Every tear and every sigh,
He gathers close, never dry.
In the stillness, we lay our fears,
The gentle whisper dries our tears.

In the breaking dawn, hope appears,
Filling our hearts, calming our fears.
A sacred bond, eternally true,
The gentle whispers speak of you.

With every heartbeat, we trust and grow,
Through valleys deep, through rivers flow.
Faith guides our steps, at every turn,
In whispers soft, His love we learn.

## **Climbing the Ladder of Hope**

With faith as our anchor, we ascend,
Each rung of grace, our hearts commend.
Climbing higher, with every prayer,
Towards the heavens, our spirits flare.

With every struggle, we find our strength,
In unity, we traverse great length.
The ladder reaches to skies above,
In every step, we feel His love.

Our burdens lifted, we rise as one,
In trials and triumphs, His will be done.
Each heartbeat echoes, a testament true,
Climbing the ladder, we make it through.

The summit glows with promises bright,
In the presence of love, we find delight.
Through every challenge, His hand we hold,
Climbing onward, brave and bold.

From lowest valleys to the heights of grace,
In every moment, we seek His face.
With hope as our guide, we'll never fall,
On this ladder of faith, we answer His call.

# Quiet Footfalls on Sacred Ground

In quiet moments, our spirits rise,
With every footfall, we touch the skies.
On sacred ground, we gather near,
The echoes of love, we long to hear.

Each step in faith, a pilgrimage made,
Through fields of grace, in Him we're laid.
A tapestry woven with threads of light,
On sacred ground, we find our sight.

With hearts as candles, burning bright,
We share the warmth, dispelling night.
In gentle whispers, His truth we seek,
On quiet footfalls, our souls grow meek.

Though trials may come, we stand secure,
In the promise of love, forever pure.
With humble hearts, we bow and bend,
On sacred ground, our souls ascend.

In unity, we walk as one,
With every dawn, a new day begun.
Quiet footfalls beckon the divine,
In this sacred space, our spirits shine.

## Each Breath a Sacred Passage

In every breath, a prayer conceived,
A silent whisper, softly received.
The essence of life flows through the soul,
Binding each heart, making us whole.

With each inhale, peace we embrace,
In exhale, we find our sacred place.
The rhythm of life, a dance divine,
In every heartbeat, love's pure sign.

Awakened in grace, we shall rise,
Breath by breath, we touch the skies.
Moments of stillness, pure and bright,
Each breath a passage, guiding the light.

Through trials faced, we breathe with trust,
In sacred whispers, a promise, a must.
For in this journey, sacred and vast,
Each breath we take, a bond that will last.

So cherish the moments, both near and far,
For each breath we take, is our brightest star.
In the tapestry woven with love and care,
Each breath a passage, a treasure so rare.

## Moments Woven in Divine Light

In fleeting moments, we find our grace,
Woven together in time and space.
Threads of connection, bright and bold,
In each heartbeat, a story told.

Divine light shines on paths we tread,
In the gentle whispers, love is spread.
Every glance, a glimpse of the divine,
Moments shared, eternally shine.

Within the silence, we hear the call,
The sacred echo that binds us all.
In laughter and tears, the spirits meet,
In divine light, our hearts find beat.

Each sunset paints the canvas bright,
With colors infused by heavenly light.
Moments woven, a sacred thread,
In every encounter, love is spread.

So cherish each second, fleeting yet bright,
For in these moments, we're wrapped in light.
Together we walk, hand in hand,
In moments woven, forever we stand.

## **Trusting the Unfolding Path**

Footsteps taken on unknown ground,
In trust we move, with love profound.
The path unfolds beneath our feet,
In every turn, a lesson sweet.

With open hearts, we face the day,
In shadows cast, we find our way.
Though storms may rise, and doubts arise,
In trusting the path, our spirit flies.

Each struggle faced, a stepping stone,
Leading to places we've never known.
With faith as our guide, we seek the light,
Trusting the journey, both day and night.

Indecision fades, as courage steers,
With every breath, we shed our fears.
In the unfolding, grace reveals,
The beauty of what our heart truly feels.

So forward we go, hand in hand,
On paths we trust, our futures planned.
In the journey's weave, we find our part,
Trusting the unfolding, matters of the heart.

## The Faithful Traveler's Trail

With each new dawn, the traveler wakes,
Guided by faith, no matter what breaks.
Steps may falter, yet hope prevails,
On this journey, the heart never pales.

Through valleys deep and mountains high,
In every moment, the spirit flies.
With eyes wide open, we seek and find,
The faithful trail that binds mankind.

Companions met along the way,
Their laughter and love, brightens the day.
In unity, our souls entwine,
Each traveler's tale, a sacred sign.

The map of life is drawn in grace,
Through trials and joys, we find our place.
With every challenge, lessons unfold,
The faithful traveler's heart remains bold.

So walk together, hand in hand,
On the sacred trail, across the land.
In the beauty of journey, we will prevail,
For we are one on the faithful trail.

## The Graceful March of the Hopeful

In the dawn's soft, glowing light,
Faithful hearts take to the flight.
Guided by the stars above,
Marching onward with pure love.

Through valleys deep and mountains high,
They lift their voices to the sky.
Each step a prayer, a whispered plea,
In unity, they walk so free.

The burdens of the world they share,
In every trial, strength laid bare.
Hope ignites the path they tread,
With grace alive, while shadows fled.

As rivers flow, they journey forth,
A testament of unwavering worth.
In faith and trust, their spirits rise,
Bound to the heavens, the great skies.

Together, they embrace the way,
In every dawn, a new display.
With hearts entwined, they sing their song,
In grace they gather, bold and strong.

## Listening to the Quiet Calls

In stillness found, the spirit speaks,
Soft whispers calm, and love it seeks.
Among the trees, a gentle breeze,
Cradles thoughts, as time will freeze.

Each rustling leaf, a sacred sound,
In nature's arms, peace is found.
Hearts attune to the silent choir,
Echoes of hope, lifting higher.

In quiet moments, truth reveals,
Wisdom in the way it feels.
Every sigh, a sacred chance,
To take the path of faith's dance.

As stars align in night's embrace,
Each twinkling light, a dash of grace.
Listening close, a still, small voice,
Guides the journey, leads the choice.

In humble prayer, we gently kneel,
Sensing love that time can heal.
Within the silence, hearts will grow,
To listen deeply, truth will flow.

# The Gentle Turns of Life

Life's journey weaves, a sacred dress,
With seams of joy and threads of stress.
Each gentle turn, a lesson learned,
In warmth and light our spirits burned.

With every dawn, new paths appear,
Embracing change, we conquer fear.
In every season, growth unfolds,
Through trials faced, our story's told.

The rivers twist, the mountains sway,
Yet faith remains, a guiding ray.
In laughter's echo, and sorrow's cry,
Life's delicate dance, we cannot deny.

Through open hearts, we find our way,
Each gentle turn, a bright array.
Embracing faith, we carry on,
With hope as light, till shadows gone.

In every breath, a chance to start,
To share our love, to open heart.
For in each turn, a promise thrives,
In gentle love, the spirit lives.

## Grace in Each Footfall

In quiet paths where shadows play,
Soft whispers guide our weary way.
With every step, a prayer unfurled,
In grace we dance, through this wide world.

Angels tread where our hearts abide,
In love's embrace, we do not hide.
Through stormy seas and tranquil nights,
His light shall lead, our souls ignites.

Each footfall echoes heaven's song,
In sacred trust, we do belong.
Through trials faced and joys we find,
A perfect peace within, we bind.

Our journey wrought with faith's pure thread,
His mercy flows where angels tread.
In every moment, pure and bright,
In grace we move, towards the light.

So let us walk in humble awe,
With hearts attuned to every law.
For in each step, may we behold,
The grace that fills our hearts of gold.

## **The Holy Trek Unfolds**

On sacred paths, our journey weaves,
With every step, the heart believes.
Through valleys vast, and mountains steep,
We seek the truth, our souls to keep.

As daylight glows, the shadows flee,
In faith, we walk, eternally free.
On holy ground, our spirits soar,
In every breath, we seek for more.

The skies above, a canvas bright,
Each star a beacon, guiding light.
Together bound, our voices rise,
In unity, we touch the skies.

Through storms and trials, we remain,
In love and grace, we bear the strain.
Each challenge faced, a chance to grow,
In holy joy, our spirits flow.

So onward, upward, we shall tread,
With every prayer, our lives are fed.
The holy trek, a path divine,
In every heartbeat, grace will shine.

## Walking the Divine Way

Upon the path where angels soar,
We seek the truth, forevermore.
With every breath, we hope to see,
The guiding hand that sets us free.

In gentle fields where flowers bloom,
We hear His voice disperse the gloom.
Each sacred moment, pure and sweet,
Reveals the journey as we meet.

As sun and moon embrace the sky,
We walk the way with spirits high.
With faith as light, we find our quest,
In every trial, we are blessed.

His whispers dance upon the air,
In every heart, He finds a share.
Amongst the trials, joy we glean,
In steps of love, His paths are seen.

Hand in hand with grace we tread,
On holy ground where dreams are fed.
With each step, the truth we share,
In Him alone, we find our care.

## **Embracing the Heavenly Rhythm**

In sacred time, the clock's refrain,
We find our peace amidst the pain.
With open hearts, we sway and flow,
To heavenly rhythms that bestow.

Each heartbeat sings of ancient grace,
A symphony in every space.
Through trials vast and joys untold,
His love flows fiercely, brave and bold.

The universe in harmony,
With every step, we're set to see.
In every breath, a note divine,
A gift bestowed, a love that shines.

Through dawn's embrace and twilight's art,
We dance with faith that stirs the heart.
In nature's pulse, we hear the call,
For love unites and lifts us all.

So let us sway in unity,
In every soul, a melody.
For in this dance, we rise and sing,
Embracing grace in everything.

## The Slow Dance of Devotion

In stillness found, our hearts align,
We share the space of love divine.
With gentle steps, we move as one,
In sacred rhythm 'til day is done.

Each moment lingers, pure and true,
With every glance, the spirit's view.
Amidst the quiet, prayers take flight,
In slow devotion, pure delight.

As shadows whisper, we greet the dawn,
With open arms, a new day drawn.
In every pause, His grace we find,
A holy bond that ties the blind.

So let us waltz on faith's sweet breeze,
In gentle trust, our souls at ease.
For in this dance of hearts so bold,
We weave our stories, love unfolds.

Through every twirl and step we take,
In love's embrace, hearts never break.
For in slow dance, our spirits rise,
In sacred trust, we touch the skies.

## From Dust to Divine

From dust we rise, a humble start,
In sacred breath, the beating heart.
With hands uplifted, we seek the light,
In faith we soar, on wings of might.

With every trial, we find our grace,
In moments still, we seek His face.
From shadows deep, to heights above,
Transformed by mercy, wrapped in love.

In whispered prayers, our spirits blend,
A journey woven, with no end.
In trials faced, we learn to be,
Reflections of divinity.

With every step, a path unfolds,
In sacred stories, life retold.
From dust to stars, we're called to rise,
Embracing truth, we touch the skies.

Oh, may our hearts forever seek,
In gentle whispers, love will speak.
As souls unite, no longer blind,
Together we'll ascend, entwined.

## Awakening in Every Step

With every step, the earth we tread,
In softened soil, His promise spread.
Awakening hearts, the spirit calls,
In every moment, His love enthralls.

In breath of life, the journey starts,
As we embrace the holy arts.
With open eyes, we search the skies,
In faithful hearts, the truth shall rise.

The whispered winds, a guiding hand,
In every heartbeat, we understand.
In acts of kindness, we find our way,
Awakening souls, come what may.

With joy in tears, through every plight,
In darkness faced, we seek the light.
Step by step, we rise anew,
In grace we walk, our spirits true.

Together we dance, in rhythm divine,
In love's embrace, our hearts align.
Awakening minds, in every step,
In sacred trust, our lives adept.

## Eternity Beckons from Afar

Eternity calls, a distant shore,
In silence deep, we yearn for more.
With every heartbeat, we feel the pull,
A promise whispered, our spirits full.

In twilight's glow, our hopes resound,
As faith unfolds, our hearts unbound.
The stars above, a guiding chart,
Illuminating the sacred heart.

In moments fleeting, we touch the divine,
A glimpse of love, where souls entwine.
With every tear, we learn to see,
Eternity beckons, setting us free.

Through trials faced, we rise and shine,
In unity found, the truth's design.
With every prayer, we journey near,
In sacred bonds, we cast out fear.

Forever seeking, we strive to know,
As boundless love begins to flow.
Eternity waits, with arms extended,
In the sacred dance, lives blended.

## The Steps that Lead Us Home

The steps we take, a journey blessed,
In search of peace, our hearts find rest.
With faith as guide, through storms we roam,
In unison sought, we find our home.

With each embrace, the world transforms,
In sacred touch, our spirit warms.
In gentle whispers, love appears,
The path of healing, washed in tears.

As we surrender, to His embrace,
Our feet are led to sacred space.
In hope ignited, we rise in grace,
The steps that lead, through time and place.

Oh, may our hearts in rhythm beat,
As barriers fall, in love we meet.
With every journey, our souls ignite,
The steps that lead us into light.

Together we wander, hand in hand,
In every heartbeat, we understand.
The way is clear, when love is shown,
The steps that lead, will guide us home.

## **The Sacred Path of Patience**

In silence, wisdom grows,
With every step, we pause.
Faith beckons from the shadows,
Guiding hearts to gentle cause.

Seasons change, yet we stand still,
In trust we find our way.
Each moment a divine will,
Patient souls shall not sway.

With nature's hand, we whisper,
Lessons carved in stone.
Patience, our steadfast sister,
Leading us to the throne.

Beneath the stars, we gather,
Unity in our song.
Through trials, we'll not falter,
In patience, we grow strong.

So tread this sacred pathway,
With hearts both light and true.
For every step that we may take,
Brings us closer to you.

## Progress Through Prayer

In humble whispers, we begin,
Voices raised to the sky.
With open hearts, we seek within,
To mend the soul's reply.

Each prayer a beacon, shining bright,
Through darkness, hope shall soar.
Together, we embrace the light,
In unity, we explore.

With every tear, a seed is sown,
Faith blossoms on the ground.
In solitude, we've not alone,
For love is always found.

Beneath the weight of silent nights,
Our spirits dance and rise.
In grace, we find our guiding lights,
Reflections in the skies.

Through prayer, our burdens lift,
In joy, we start anew.
Each moment, a sacred gift,
Connecting me to you.

**In Each Movement, a Testament**

Every breath, a sacred call,
In rhythm, hearts align.
With every rise, we stand tall,
Each moment, pure divine.

In stillness, echoes of the past,
Whispers from those who came.
Their stories, woven, hold fast,
In movement, we proclaim.

Hands uplifted to the sun,
Gratitude flows like streams.
In this dance, we are one,
Embracing holy dreams.

With every step upon this earth,
A testament we share.
In every heartbeat, we find worth,
An answer to our prayer.

So let us move as one today,
In love, our spirits mend.
In each movement, we display,
A path that has no end.

## **The Quiet March of the Faithful**

In shadows deep, the faithful tread,
With quiet strength, they rise.
Each heart aflame, no words are said,
Yet hope ignites the skies.

Through valleys low and mountains high,
They journey side by side.
With every step, they testify,
In faith they shall abide.

Their burdens shared in silent grace,
A bond that will not break.
In every challenge, they embrace,
The love that they awake.

With every prayer, the echoes swell,
A harmony divine.
In quiet hearts, peace will dwell,
As stars in darkness shine.

So march, oh faithful, through the night,
With courage in your hands.
In unity, we'll find the light,
As love forever stands.

## Sacred Paths Underfoot

Upon the earth, where shadows fall,
We tread the paths, Heeding the call.
In whispers soft, the spirit speaks,
Guiding the heart, where faith seeks.

With every step, a prayer unfolds,
In sacred trust, our story holds.
Through trials faced, and lessons learned,
The light of love forever burned.

The mountains high, the valleys wide,
In every trial, we abide.
For every stone that meets our shoe,
A blessing comes, a vision true.

Beneath the stars, the night divine,
We find our strength, in love we shine.
Through sacred paths, and sacred ties,
We walk with hope, we rise, we rise.

In unity, our souls awake,
With every breath, we silence ache.
Together bound, we forge a way,
On sacred ground, we kneel and pray.

## **Embracing the Unknown Journey**

In twilight's glow, we start to roam,
Across the lands, we'll find our home.
With every dawn, new hope flows,
In the unknown, our spirit grows.

Each step we take, a chance to learn,
Through shadows deep, and twists that turn.
With open hearts, we face the storm,
In faith we trust, and love keeps warm.

The road ahead, both wild and wide,
With courage strong, we shall not hide.
For in the dark, the stars align,
Guiding our hearts, in love we shine.

With prayers as lanterns, lighting the way,
Through uncharted paths, we boldly stay.
With every breath, we seek the light,
In faith's embrace, we conquer night.

Together we stand, no fear or doubt,
In the unknown, we learn to shout.
With open arms, we greet the day,
Embracing the journey, come what may.

## The Captain of Our Souls

In seas of chaos, we find our guide,
With faith as compass, no need to hide.
Through tempests fierce, He holds us close,
The captain calm, amidst the most.

With each wave crashing, we trust the plan,
In trials faced, we're more than man.
From shores of doubt, to distant lands,
He leads the hearts, with gentle hands.

With sails unfurled, we catch the breeze,
In harmony sought, our souls at ease.
Together we navigate the night,
In His embrace, we find our light.

The horizon beckons, a promise new,
In every storm, His love shines through.
The journey's long, yet we remain,
Guided by grace, through joy and pain.

So here we stand, with hope in sight,
With faith unwavering, we rise in flight.
The captain leads, our hearts attune,
Forever anchored, we'll reach the moon.

## **In the Footprints of the Divine**

In silent prayer beneath the skies,
We walk where earthly shadows lie.
Each step a whisper, each breath a grace,
In the footprints of the Divine we trace.

The sun it rises, casting light,
Guiding hearts through the deep of night.
With every tear, a healing song,
In love's embrace, we all belong.

Mountains tremble, valleys sing,
Nature praises the Creator's wing.
Through storm and calm, His will shall reign,
In the footprints of joy and pain.

In the mirror of each soul's face,
We find reflections of His grace.
United in purpose, we rise above,
In the footprints of eternal love.

The journey leads us to the throne,
Where faith is sown and hope is grown.
In every heart, His light will shine,
As we walk in the footprints divine.

## Ascending the Hills of Blessing

Come, climb with me the sacred heights,
Where blessings dance in golden lights.
With open hearts, we seek His face,
Ascending the hills of love and grace.

Each step we take, a prayer we send,
To touch the heavens, our spirits mend.
The breeze declares His gentle might,
In every dawn and every night.

With valleys deep and skies so wide,
In faith's embrace, we shall abide.
The past behind, our eyes ahead,
On the hills of blessing, we are led.

The echoes of joy, the songs of peace,
In His embrace, our doubts release.
Through trials vast, we find our way,
Ascending to greet the light of day.

Together we rise, through storm and calm,
In the hills of blessing, find the balm.
With hearts entwined and voices high,
Ascending to where our hopes can fly.

## The Slow Unfolding of Truth

In the quiet moments, still and clear,
The heart unfolds what it holds dear.
With patience borne of gentle hands,
The slow unfolding of truth expands.

Each doubt transformed, a testament,
Of faith in trials, the soul unbent.
In every tear, a lesson learned,
The slow unfolding, as wisdom yearned.

Through shadowed paths and light so bright,
In the tapestry of day and night.
Threads of doubt come to a close,
The slow unfolding, the spirit grows.

With every heartbeat, whispers come,
To guide us gently, to lead us home.
In the stillness, truth will bloom,
The slow unfolding dispels all gloom.

So let us walk this sacred way,
Embracing truths that softly sway.
Together we rise to forge what's true,
In the slow unfolding, love shines through.

## A Journey Anchored in the Spirit

With faith as sail and love as guide,
A journey anchored in the Spirit wide.
Through tempest winds and tranquil seas,
In the heart's embrace, we find our ease.

Each tide that rises teaches grace,
With every wave comes a holy place.
Anchored deep in joy's embrace,
A journey guided by His face.

In the whispers of the morning light,
We find our strength to face the night.
With open hearts, let's share the load,
On this journey, we shall code.

Together we wander, hand in hand,
In unity's firm, unwavering stand.
Through valleys low and mountains steep,
A journey anchored, His promises keep.

For when the storms of life assail,
With faith as our compass, we shall prevail.
In every moment, near or far,
A journey anchored beneath His star.

## **Threads of Devotion Stitching Time**

In silent whispers, prayers arise,
Each bead a moment, in cosmic ties.
Threads of faith woven, strong and bright,
Stitching our hearts to eternal light.

Beneath the sun, in night's embrace,
We seek the touch of sacred grace.
With every stitch, a promise made,
In this divine tapestry laid.

Through joy and sorrow, love doth sew,
A sacred bond in ebb and flow.
Each life a strand, each soul a part,
Together they weave the one true heart.

With hands united, we craft our fate,
In the loom of time, we contemplate.
Threads of devotion, stitched with care,
In the fabric of life, we find our prayer.

As seasons change, and years roll by,
Our spirits soar, like birds on high.
In each moment, a chance to find,
The sacred thread that binds mankind.

## A Pilgrimage Through the Heart

Upon the path where shadows dance,
A journey beckons, a holy chance.
With every step, our souls align,
On sacred ground, where stars do shine.

Through valleys deep and mountains high,
We follow whispers, a fervent sigh.
In valleys lush, or deserts bare,
Our hearts, like compasses, lead with care.

In moments still, we seek the wise,
Finding truth in the boundless skies.
Each heartbeat echoes, a sacred song,
In unity's embrace, we all belong.

With open hearts, we share our fears,
Turning each sorrow into tears.
On this pilgrimage, we grow anew,
In every blessing, love shines through.

As nights dissolve into dawn's soft glow,
Faith becomes the light we know.
Through every challenge, every turn,
In our hearts, the flame will burn.

## A Sacred Journey Unfolding

Beneath the stars on starlit plains,
We walk in faith, shedding our chains.
Each step a prayer, and every breath,
Carving our souls 'til the end of death.

The moonlight guides our silent quest,
In hidden paths, we seek our rest.
With every heartbeat, a promise glows,
In the river of life, our spirit flows.

In sacred whispers, we hear the call,
A symphony of love, embracing all.
Each moment precious, each touch divine,
In the heart's garden, we intertwine.

Through trials faced and mountains climbed,
In unity's light, our spirits rhymed.
The journey unfolds, a map of grace,
We walk hand in hand in this holy space.

With every sunrise, hope will rise,
In trusting our hearts and open skies.
A sacred journey, we'll boldly share,
Together we find our way to prayer.

## The Path of Faithful Tread

Upon the road where many tread,
A testament to the words once said.
With every footstep, we leave our mark,
As we journey forth, guided from the dark.

In the forest deep, the whispers call,
Echoes of wisdom from ancients all.
Each leaf a lesson, each branch a guide,
In nature's arms, we find our stride.

The sun might wane, and shadows grow,
But in our hearts, the fire will glow.
With steadfast love, we face the night,
As hope's bright light stirs us to fight.

Together we walk, through grief and cheer,
In every moment, your presence near.
The path of the faithful, woven tight,
Through trials and triumphs, we find our light.

In unity's strength, we rise as one,
Each step we take, a race well-run.
With open hearts and courage spread,
We light the way where the faithful tread.

## Navigating the Fog of Doubt

In shadows deep, where faith may wane,
We seek the light, yet feel the strain.
With every step, we lose our way,
Yet hope's soft whisper guides the fray.

In silence loud, our questions rise,
Like fragile dreams beneath the skies.
But trust in grace leads hearts to mend,
As doubt surrenders to the bend.

The fog may thicken, the path unclear,
But in our souls, Your voice we hear.
Each tear we shed, a seed is sown,
In fertile ground, our faith has grown.

With courage bold, we face the night,
For every heart seeks out the light.
Through trials faced and battles won,
Our spirits soar, with joy begun.

So let the fog be ever near,
In darkest paths, we persevere.
For He who calls us from the deep,
Will hold our hands as we awake from sleep.

## The Serenity of Slow Movements

In quietude, the heart must rest,
Amidst the rush, we are most blessed.
Each gentle breath, a sacred pause,
Reveals the truth, reveals the cause.

With mindful steps, we tread the earth,
In every moment, find rebirth.
The weight of time slows weary minds,
As grace and peace in stillness bind.

In every leaf that flutters down,
Is whispered love, a sacred crown.
Embrace the dawn with open hand,
In holy rhythms, we understand.

Through sacred space, our spirits dance,
In nature's arms, we take a chance.
The gentle flow of life's sweet stream,
Invites our souls to drift and dream.

As stars align, in cosmic flow,
We find our place, we learn to grow.
In slowing down, we realize,
That in our hearts, the truth defies.

## Soulful Footprints in the Sand

With every step upon the shore,
We leave behind what was before.
Each mark a tale, a life embraced,
In grains of time, our souls are traced.

The tide may rise and wash away,
Yet in the heart, these footprints stay.
In every grain, a memory lives,
A silent call, as spirit gives.

In sunlit paths and stormy skies,
Our journeys marked with silent sighs.
As footprints blend with ocean's hand,
We walk with Him upon the sand.

With every wave that breaks anew,
We find the love that we pursue.
For in this dance of ebb and flow,
Our souls unite, our spirits grow.

So let us walk this vast expanse,
In spirit's grace, we take our chance.
For every step beneath the sun,
Is where our souls and love are spun.

## **Lanterns Lighting the Way**

In darkest nights, our paths are fraught,
Yet lanterns glow, with love they've sought.
Each flicker bright, a guiding spark,
To illuminate the endless dark.

With hearts aglow, we share the flame,
As kindred souls call out His name.
Together borne, by hope and grace,
We light the way, our fears erase.

In every shadow, in every doubt,
These lanterns lit, we move about.
For when we join, in love's embrace,
The path ahead becomes our place.

With faith ablaze, we stand as one,
In this great light, our work begun.
With every step, the world we change,
As love ignites the hearts, estranged.

So let us carry forth this glow,
Illuminate the hearts, we know.
For in the darkness, love will stay,
Our lanterns bright, to guide the way.

## **One Breath, One Praise**

In quiet whispers, we begin,
A sacred moment, hearts within.
With every breath, a prayer takes flight,
One praise resounds, through day and night.

In dawn's embrace, we lift our voice,
In gratitude, we make our choice.
Each heartbeat echoes joy and grace,
In unity, we seek Your face.

The gentle breeze, a holy sign,
In nature's beauty, love divine.
With open hands, we share the light,
One breath, one praise, our souls unite.

Through trials faced, we find our strength,
In love's embrace, we go the length.
For in the silence, Your truth calls,
One breath, one heart, the Spirit sprawls.

In every moment, hope we find,
A melody that binds mankind.
With every breath, we rise, we soar,
One praise forever, evermore.

## Walking the Labyrinth of Faith

Along the winding path we tread,
With quiet steps, our spirits led.
In shadows deep, Your light we seek,
In every turn, Your voice we speak.

Each twist and turn, a thought made clear,
With every breath, we draw You near.
Though doubts may rise, we hold our ground,
In silence, Lord, Your love is found.

Through trials faced, we gain our sight,
With gentle grace, we seek the right.
In labyrinths of doubt and grace,
We find, dear Lord, our sacred space.

With faith as guide, our spirits rise,
In every tear, joy's sweet surprise.
Together, Lord, we walk this road,
In trust, we share this heavy load.

In labyrinth's heart, we find our way,
In every night, there comes the day.
Your hand in mine, I take each stride,
In faith, O Lord, I shall abide.

# A Journey in Divine Rhythm

In morning's light, we start to roam,
With every beat, we find our home.
The rhythm of Your love untold,
In heartbeats warm, our faith unfolds.

Through valleys low and mountains high,
With every tear, we learn to fly.
Your melody, a gentle thread,
In every note, our souls are fed.

Each moment, Lord, we hear Your song,
In harmony, we all belong.
With open hearts, we dance and sway,
In divine rhythm, guide our way.

Through storms that rage and calm that stays,
Your presence shines, a beacon's rays.
In every challenge, we find grace,
With steps in time, we run this race.

As night descends, the stars align,
In cosmic dance, Your love is mine.
Forever in this rhythm dwell,
A journey, Lord, we know so well.

## Each Step, A New Revelation

With every step upon this ground,
A new revelation can be found.
In faith we walk, though blind we see,
Your guiding light will set us free.

Through trials faced, we gain our strength,
Each moment lived reveals the length.
For in the depths of sorrow's night,
We find in You our source of light.

The path may twist, but never strays,
In every heart, Your warmth conveys.
As faith unfolds, we learn to trust,
In every challenge, rise we must.

Each step we take, in joy or pain,
Your love remains, a sweet refrain.
In sacred stillness, we embrace,
The gifts of truth in every place.

With every breath, new visions bloom,
Illumined paths dispel all gloom.
In each step, we cherish grace,
With open hearts, we seek Your face.

## Under His Watchful Gaze

In the stillness of the night,
I feel His presence near,
A gentle whisper in the dark,
Calming every fear.

Beneath the endless sky above,
His love will never cease,
With every star a promise made,
A beacon of His peace.

In shadows deep, He guides my soul,
Through valleys where I tread,
His light, a lamp along my path,
In Him, I'm truly led.

Each morning brings His grace anew,
A chance to rise and soar,
With faith as strong as mountain stone,
I walk through every door.

Under His watchful gaze I dwell,
In love, I place my trust,
For with Him by my side I know,
In Him, I'm always just.

## With Faith in My Soles

With faith in my soles, I walk this way,
Each step a prayer, each moment a sway.
The road is long, but fear stays behind,
In every heartbeat, His love I find.

Through trials and storms, I march with grace,
Carrying light in this sacred space.
No burden too heavy, no shadow too cold,
With faith in my soles, I am truly bold.

The whispers of doubt may try to entwine,
But I stand firm, for His will is divine.
With courage ignited, I journey on,
In Him, I am anchored, my fears all gone.

In each step forward, He walks beside,
An unyielding presence, my faithful guide.
With faith in my soles, I rise and shine,
In this dance of life, His heart aligns.

Across the land, my spirit shall roam,
With faith in my soles, I'm never alone.
For every journey is blessed and bright,
In the warmth of His love, I find my light.

## The Unfolding Prayer

In the morning light, my heart takes flight,
With an unfolding prayer that feels so right.
Each word a seed, sown deep in the ground,
In the garden of faith, where love is found.

As petals unfurl, my spirit awakes,
With each gentle whisper, a promise He makes.
The silence speaks volumes, the stillness sings,
In the sacred space, true joy it brings.

Night's shadows may gather, but hope shines clear,
In every heartbeat, my Savior is near.
With each breath I take, I feel Him unfold,
The warmth of His presence, a story retold.

In patience I wait, as the leaves turn bright,
Trusting His timing, embracing the light.
With the trust of a child, I lift up my voice,
In the poem of life, He's the heart of my choice.

The unfolding prayer brings peace and grace,
In the tapestry woven, I find my place.
With faith as my anchor, I rise from despair,
In the heart of His love, I find solace there.

# Light for Every Journey

Light for every journey, shining bright,
Guiding my steps through the darkest night.
With faith as my compass, hope in my chest,
I navigate life, trust leading the rest.

Each moment a gift, each lesson divine,
In the warmth of His presence, my heart aligns.
With every dawn breaking, grace fills the air,
He lights up my path; I'm free from despair.

When storms may rage and shadows fall near,
I hold fast to courage, dispelling the fear.
His promise, a lantern, unwavering and true,
In the voyage of life, I'm led by His view.

Through valleys of doubt and mountains of grace,
In the arms of the Father, I find my place.
With light for each journey, my soul takes flight,
With faith as my guide, I embrace the light.

Each step filled with purpose, my spirit set free,
In the laughter of love, I discover the key.
For light for every journey is forged in His love,
A celestial beacon, sent down from above.

**Stepwise toward the Infinite**

In whispers soft, the path unfolds,
Each step a prayer, each thought a mold.
With faith as guide, we move ahead,
Toward realms where angels softly tread.

The stars above, they shine so bright,
Pointing the way through deepest night.
In every struggle, grace will bloom,
A testament to love's great room.

The heart beats strong, with hope's embrace,
In trials faced, we find our place.
With every heartbeat, closer still,
To endless joy, to boundless will.

Where visions blend, and dreams take flight,
We seek the dawn from depths of night.
A journey shared, a sacred trust,
In unity, we rise from dust.

So step by step, we pave the road,
With souls aflame, we bear the load.
Each turn reveals what lies beyond,
The Infinite awaits, a holy bond.

## **The Quiet Resilience of Faith**

In silence deep, the spirit grows,
A seed of love that gently glows.
Through trials fierce, it bends but stands,
A testament of unseen hands.

The storm may howl, the shadows creep,
Yet in our hearts, a promise keeps.
With unwavering strength, we rise anew,
In every breath, our faith rings true.

The quiet voice that soothes the soul,
Leads us onward, makes us whole.
In weary moments, trust takes flight,
A beacon shining in the night.

Though doubts may dance, and fears collide,
In faith, we stand, with hearts open wide.
Together we forge a brighter way,
A path of light, come what may.

For love prevails, through darkest days,
A melody of gentle praise.
With quiet strength, we carry on,
In every struggle, we are reborn.

## The Harmony of Progress

In steps of hope, we find our voice,
Together we rise, in love rejoice.
With every action, a seed is sown,
In unity's strength, our spirits grown.

The rhythm flows, a sacred dance,
In each heartbeat lies a chance.
With visions clear, we shape the day,
In harmony, we will not sway.

Through trials faced, together stand,
With open hearts, we build this land.
A tapestry of dreams entwined,
With threads of faith, our fates aligned.

The journey calls, we heed the sound,
In every heartbeat, grace is found.
For in the struggle, beauty grows,
A world transformed, a love that flows.

So side by side, we venture forth,
In every corner of the earth.
With hope ablaze, we tides will shift,
In progress made, we find our gift.

## A Trail Lit by Love

In the light of dawn, love casts its glow,
A trail unfolds, where hearts do flow.
With every step, a promise made,
In love's embrace, our fears will fade.

Through winding paths, with joy we'll tread,
With open hearts, we're gently led.
In every smile, in every tear,
Together we forge a bond that's clear.

The echoes of laughter fill the air,
In love's sweet harmony, we share.
With grateful hearts, we walk as one,
In every moment, a chance begun.

Through shadows deep, our light will shine,
A beacon bright, a love divine.
With every heartbeat, we will stand,
In unity, we clasp each hand.

So let us walk this sacred trail,
In love's embrace, we shall not fail.
For where we go, hope's light shall beam,
A path of joy, a shared dream.

## The Faithful Ascent

We rise on paths of light and grace,
With hands uplifted, hearts embrace.
Each step we take, with faith we climb,
Finding our way, in seeking time.

In trials faced, we find our might,
With every day, we walk in light.
The mountain high, our spirits soar,
In holy whispers, we implore.

Through valleys deep, we seek the truth,
In every moment, the face of youth.
The faithful hands, we lend and share,
In love's embrace, we cast our care.

As dawn breaks forth, the shadows flee,
With eyes of hope, we choose to see.
Our burdens lift, with voices raised,
In unity, we sing our praise.

Each summit reached, our spirits free,
In sacred space, we find the key.
So onward now, to greater heights,
The faithful ascent, our hearts ignite.

## In Serenity We Walk

In quiet moments, we find our peace,
Within the stillness, anxieties cease.
Each step we take, in gentle flow,
The light of love will always show.

With every breath, we feel His grace,
In nature's arms, we find our place.
The winds may shift, yet faith will stay,
In serenity, we find our way.

Among the trees, His whispers call,
In sacred spaces, we give our all.
With open hearts, we hear the sound,
A tranquil path, where love abounds.

The sun's soft glow, a guiding light,
We walk together, day and night.
With every stride, His presence near,
In serenity, we shed our fear.

Through trials faced, we rise anew,
With every step, we trust what's true.
In harmony, our spirits blend,
In serenity, our journey bends.

## **The Map of His Love**

In pages worn, the truth unfolds,
A sacred map of love retold.
With every line, a path so clear,
In God's embrace, we know no fear.

Through valleys low and mountains steep,
His love surrounds, in silence deep.
Each marker holds, a guiding star,
With faith as our compass, we'll go far.

In moments lost, when shadows play,
His love illuminates the way.
With tender hands, He draws us near,
In every heartbeat, He is here.

Through stormy seas, we feel His hand,
In trusting hearts, together stand.
The map of life, drawn with His care,
In every journey, love laid bare.

So follow well, the lines He's drawn,
In every dusk, in every dawn.
With hope renewed and spirit free,
The map of His love will guide thee.

## Each Step a Prayer

With every footfall, we seek to pray,
In silent whispers, we find our way.
The ground we tread, sacred and pure,
Each step we take, our hearts endure.

In moments lost, we bow our heads,
For every doubt, in faith it spreads.
With thankful hearts, we walk this land,
Each step a prayer, in His command.

In morning light, we rise anew,
Reflecting grace in all we do.
Through trials faced, with courage bold,
Each step a prayer, a story told.

In unity, we gather near,
In every heartbeat, He is here.
With hope ablaze, our spirits soar,
Each step a prayer, forevermore.

As evening falls, and stars align,
We walk together, His love divine.
In every journey, through joy and care,
Each step a prayer, a bond we share.

## Each Breath a Blessing

With every breath, we're graced to live,
In silent gratitude, we give.
The air we share, a gift so rare,
Each breath a blessing, beyond compare.

In gentle winds, His spirit flows,
In quiet moments, His presence grows.
With every sigh, we feel His might,
Each breath a blessing, pure and bright.

Through trials faced, and sorrows known,
In every challenge, we are not alone.
With open hearts, we find the light,
Each breath a blessing, day and night.

As nature breathes, in rhythm true,
We find our strength in all we do.
With love as guide, our spirits rise,
Each breath a blessing, touching the skies.

In life's embrace, we find our song,
With every breath, we all belong.
Together bound, in unity's quest,
Each breath a blessing, forever blessed.

## With Each Breath, a New Horizon

With each breath I take, a promise unfolds,
A canvas of grace, in colors untold.
Hope dances lightly, on the edge of the light,
Inviting my heart to embrace the sweet night.

In the whispers of dawn, I hear the soft call,
A reminder that love transcends every fall.
Through valleys of shadow, faith leads me on,
With courage anew, I greet every dawn.

In the depths of my soul, a river flows bright,
A testament of trust, a beacon of light.
With gratitude flowing, on waves of pure song,
I rise with the sun, where I truly belong.

Each moment a gift, a chance to renew,
The journey we travel, forever in view.
With each breath that nourishes spirit and skin,
A horizon awakens, where love can begin.

So I walk unafraid, with grace on my side,
A pilgrim of hope, where dreams abide.
Faith's melody sings in the depth of my soul,
With each breath, a new horizon, I become whole.

# Trusting the Whisper of the Spirit

In silence I linger, where echoes arise,
The whispering Spirit, my heart's deepest prize.
With each gentle stroke, it calls me to stand,
To follow the path that is lovingly planned.

In moments of doubt, when shadows entwine,
I seek out the light, your presence divine.
Trusting in whispers that guide through the night,
A compass of hope, shining ever so bright.

When storms cloud my vision, and fears start to loom,
I breathe in your peace, and the chaos subsumes.
With each tender word, my spirit takes flight,
Wrapped in your wisdom, I find my way right.

Through valleys of sorrow and mountaintops high,
I trust in the voice that will never deny.
For even in darkness, your love will prevail,
With courage ignited, I follow the trail.

So I surrender my doubts, and hold you so near,
The whispers of Spirit dissolve every fear.
In joyous abandon, I journey ahead,
Trusting each step, my heart ever led.

## The Gentle Ascent of Belief

With faith like a seed, I climb the steep hill,
Each step is a moment, each breath is a thrill.
In valleys of wonder, on peaks bathed in light,
The gentle ascent makes my spirit feel right.

The air soft and sweet, filled with promise and grace,
I carry my burdens, yet quicken my pace.
Through trials and triumphs, my heart learns to soar,
In the whisper of hope, I seek to explore.

As I rise through the shadows, the dawn starts to break,
Awakening visions, of love that won't shake.
With each gentle cloud that I brush with my hand,
I find pieces of joy in the vastness of land.

In moments of stillness, I breathe in the truth,
That faith isn't blind, but a pathway to youth.
Belief is a journey, a song yet unsealed,
In the rhythm of life, my heart is revealed.

So I climb ever higher, with hope as my guide,
In the gentle ascent, my spirit will bide.
With the strength of conviction, I'll reach for the sky,
The gentle ascent of belief will not die.

**Footsteps on the Narrow Way**

In quiet reflection, I tread on this path,
With footsteps so humble, I seek not the wrath.
Each step that I take, a witness to grace,
A journey of love, in this sacred place.

The narrow way beckons, with whispers of peace,
A compass of light, where worries can cease.
With every intention, I soften my heart,
As kindness and mercy become my true art.

Through trials I wander, with faith as my shield,
In the depth of each struggle, my spirit is healed.
With courage I rise, when shadows arise,
For the narrow way guides me, through lows and through highs.

In communion with Spirit, my soul finds its tune,
As I dance with the stars and embrace the full moon.
With gratitude flowing, I carry the sway,
In the footsteps of love, on this narrow way.

So I walk hand in hand, with the Divine by my side,
Each moment a blessing, in the love I confide.
As I travel this journey, through night and through day,
I find joy in the footsteps on the narrow way.

Milton Keynes UK
Ingram Content Group UK Ltd.
UKHW020043271124
451585UK00012B/1021